Original title:
Alder Adventures

Copyright © 2025 Creative Arts Management OÜ
All rights reserved.

Author: Adeline Fairfax
ISBN HARDBACK: 978-1-80567-307-1
ISBN PAPERBACK: 978-1-80567-606-5

A Haven for the Brave

In a land where squirrels wear hats,
The raccoons hold meetings with chats.
They plot to steal snacks from the trees,
And dodge all the laughter on the breeze.

The brave souls trek through tangled thickets,
Fearing only squirrelly little pickets.
With dizzying spins and merry runs,
They welcome the chaos and all the funs.

A hedgehog plays tunes on a flute,
While bunnies break dance, oh so cute.
A tickle fight breaks in the shade,
As melodies of joy are played.

When twilight comes with a wink and a grin,
The butterflies gather, ready to spin.
With giggles and cheers, the night's alive,
In this haven, all dare to thrive.

The Dreamweaver's Trail

Upon the trail where giggles roam,
A snail makes a wish for a new home.
He dreams of racing, swift and spry,
But only manages to slowly sigh.

A wise old owl spins tales absurd,
Of dancing frogs and a flying bird.
The laughter echoes through the night,
As shadows play in the soft moonlight.

A jester fox prances with glee,
Wearing a crown made of daisies, you see.
He jokes with the turtles, slow but sly,
As fireflies twinkle and hover by.

With every twist, the giggles grow,
On this trail where the wild things flow.
A merry adventure, bright and spry,
In dreams and laughter, we learn to fly.

Glistening Stream Reflections

Bubbles bounce and giggle, oh so spry,
Fish wear tiny hats, swimming on by.
A frog in a tux, ready to prance,
With every splash, they join the dance.

Logs act as bridges for squirrels and more,
As they plot their next heist, beneath the oar.
Raccoons in masks steal snacks with delight,
Under the moon, they plan their night.

Beneath the Silent Boughs

Branches whisper secrets of curious gnomes,
Who steal cupcakes from picnics, making their homes.
A chipmunk in glasses reads tales from the trees,
While playful winds carry giggles and squeaks.

The owl on a branch hoots nonsense and jest,
While rabbits compete in the wildest of quests.
Ants hold a parade, all dressed in a line,
Marching to music, how silly, divine!

Shadows of the Old Grove

Gnarled roots twist like socks left behind,
As shadows twirl, revealing the kind.
A hedgehog plays poker, quite hard to believe,
While deer act like guards, not wanting to leave.

Mice don tuxedos, attending a ball,
Spinning and twirling, they're having a ball.
The moon, their disco, shines silver and bright,
As laughter and giggles fill up the night.

The Dance of the Leaves

Leaves twist and tumble, in a game of tag,
While squirrels perform with a jump and a wag.
A crow in a bowtie announces the fun,
As raccoons bring snacks when the dance has begun.

Twisting in laughter, the wind joins the play,
Giving every creature a reason to sway.
With nuts after the show, all gather to feast,
In a hilarious world, joy never ceased.

The Heartbeat of the Woodlands

In the forest, squirrels dance,
Chasing each other, what a chance.
Branches creak with each small leap,
While mushrooms giggle, secrets keep.

A fox in boots tries to look cool,
While raccoons plot, who's the fool?
All around, the trees do sway,
As critters join the wild ballet.

A deer jogs by with nose held high,
Bumping into a surprised fly.
With every step, a crunch and crack,
Nature's laughter echoes back.

When twilight falls, the owls hoot loud,
Gathering under the leafy shroud.
Together, they share jokes and tales,
While the wind carries their playful wails.

A Tonic for the Soul

In the meadow, bees sip sweet,
While bunnies hop, a joyful feat.
Dancing daisies wave from below,
As butterflies join the frolic show.

A gopher with a fancy hat,
Stumbles over a sleeping cat.
All the while, a worm takes bets,
On who's the quickest, no regrets.

Up in the sky, a crow does caw,
Watches the chaos from the straw.
Sipping nectar from blooms so bright,
Nature smiles in pure delight.

At sunset, the crickets sing along,
With frogs croaking their cheerful song.
In this wild, wacky jubilee,
Every creature finds their glee.

Reflections in the Woodland Pool

In the pond, a frog eyes his face,
Winking back in the water's grace.
A fish splashes, says, "What's the fuss?"
The frog just laughs, "To make a fuss!"

Nearby, a turtle takes his time,
While a silly duck thinks it's a crime.
He quacks a tune, but it's quite flat,
While the turtle just rolls with a spat.

The dragonflies zoom, with elegance grand,
Making the ripples dance at their command.
But a wayward lily decides to drift,
And sends the whole pond into a shift.

As moonlight glows, the scene is set,
A chorus of chirps, no room for fret.
Reflections sparkle, just like a gem,
In this lively woodland's littlehem.

Symphonies of the Swaying Branches

Breezy tunes from branches high,
Leaves perform their dance, oh my!
A woodpecker finds a beat,
While chipmunks tap in the summer heat.

With every shake, a squirrel spins,
Dodging acorns with little grins.
The wind plays tunes on the elms' strings,
As critters dance, oh what joy brings!

A family of songbirds starts to feast,
On berries, nuts, a real nice treat.
The elder tree hums a wise old song,
While the forest giggles, 'All day long.'

As daylight fades, the stars appear,
With laughter echoing, loud and clear.
A symphony born from life's delight,
Nature's humor shines so bright!

The Language of the Leaves

Whispers of green, a silly debate,
The wind tells secrets the squirrels relate.
Leaves giggle loudly, in a playful spree,
While branches sway, 'Look at me, look at me!'

A dance of the pines, a conifer ball,
Each rustle a joke, in the forest hall.
Moss-covered logs join in the fun,
They chuckle together under the sun.

A Quest for the Lost Clearing

Two friends in the woods, with maps upside down,
Chasing shadows, they wander around.
"Is it left at the tree, or right by the rock?"
They look at each other, both starting to mock.

Each step they take seems to lead them astray,
"Where's that clearing? Just lead the way!"
With laughter and giggles, off they do trot,
Forgetting the map, they are lost but not.

Song of the Lazy River

A river so slow, it sleeps through the day,
Fish joke and tumble, in a watery ballet.
"Hey there, old turtle! Why so low-key?"
"Just floating along, like a leaf, can't you see?"

Driftwood holds court, with a audience wide,
While the frogs croak out, "Enjoy the ride!"
They splash and they laugh, it's all quite absurd,
As the current hums softly, in ripples unheard.

The Umbral Wanderer

A shadowy figure, with a cloak full of jest,
Stumbling through thickets, just failing the quest.
"Where's that sunbeam? I've lost my way!"
The trees just chuckle, "You're here for the play!"

He trips on a root and lands with a thud,
"Who needs the sun when you've found a good mud?"
His laughter echoes, the forest replies,
"Keep wandering, friend, where the good humor lies!"

The Fairies' Refuge

In a glade where bright mushrooms sprout,
Fairies giggle, their laughter a route.
They flip through the air, with wings like lace,
Chasing the sunlight, a game to embrace.

One trips on a twig, oh what a sight!
He tumbles and rolls, a comical flight.
Another joins in, with a wink and a grin,
They laugh till they cry, let the fun begin!

With wands made of daisies, they cast playful spells,
Turning frogs into princes with magical yells.
"Wait, come back!" one fairy yelps in surprise,
As the frog hops away, oh how they all rise!

As twilight sets in, they dance in a line,
Under a moonbeam, their hearts intertwine.
A party of giggles in the leafy abode,
In their merry refuge, joy is bestowed.

Dappled Sunlight

In the forest where shadows play tricks,
Dappled sunlight dances, a mix of bright flicks.
Squirrels wear hats made of acorns and twine,
Scrambling up trees like they're doing fine!

A rabbit in glasses reads poems aloud,
While a hedgehog recites, proudly and loud.
The sunbeams are giggling, the leaves are aghast,
At the antics of animals having a blast!

The birds join the chorus, a cacophony sweet,
With rhythm and rhyme, they all tap their feet.
"Let's have a contest!" chirps one sparrow bright,
"To see who can sing until far into the night!"

And while the sun sets, the laughter won't cease,
As creatures find joy, their hearts full of peace.
In this dappled haven, let troubles take flight,
For tomorrow brings more of this pure delight!

Crescendo at Dawn

As dawn breaks the silence, the world starts to hum,
The critters awaken, and oh, what a drum!
A raccoon on maracas, a mouse on the flute,
They strum up a chorus, oh what a hoot!

The frogs join the band with their ribbiting song,
Croaking in harmony, they sing along strong.
With fireflies buzzing, they light up the stage,
And every creature feels giddy with sage.

A parade of the oddest, the funniest sights,
A turtle in sunglasses, a dance that ignites.
With twirls and some spins, they're the stars of the show,
As laughter erupts from the front row below.

"Encore!" all the leaves shout, shaking with glee,
As the sun rises higher, it's their grand jubilee.
In the morning's soft light, all worries are gone,
For life is a melody, a joyful dawn!

Whimsy in the Woodland Wonderland

In a woodland so wondrous, all things seem grand,
A fox with a top hat takes a stroll on the sand.
He tips it to critters, both big and quite small,
As giggles erupt through the trunks and the thrall.

Two bears in a hammock each take a fine nap,
But one rolls away, oh what a mishap!
He lands in a bush, with a sneeze and a shake,
And all of the wildlife start laughing, awake!

A skunk wears a bow tie, the squirrels cheer loud,
As the woodland hosts a very silly crowd.
They waltz in a circle, with acorns in hand,
For nothing can stop this fun woodland band!

As the sun sets on antics, laughter fills the air,
With friends all around, there's joy everywhere.
In this realm of delight, where whimsy runs free,
The woodland's a circus, come join it, decree!

Whispers of the Wandering Woods

In the woods, where squirrels play,
Frogs in hats dance the day away.
Trees giggle as breezes tickle,
While raccoons juggle with a pickle.

A fox wears shoes that are too tight,
He trips and tumbles, what a sight!
The owl hoots with a silly grin,
As butterflies join the playful din.

A hedgehog thinks he's quite a star,
Singing loudly, but off key by far.
The brook laughs as it splashes along,
Holding the tune to the woodland song.

At dusk, the critters gather 'round,
With stories of mischief, laughter abound.
They toast marshmallows on a stick,
Creating magic, with one funny flick.

The Secret Grove Beneath the Canopy

Deep in the grove, a secret troop,
Pinecones dance in a wiggly loop.
Mice wearing ties spin and twirl,
While ladybugs twinkle and whirl.

The raccoon chef brews acorn stew,
Served with mushrooms, oh so blue!
But oops, he spills it on his tail,
And giggles ensue as he starts to wail.

A plump rabbit hops in with flair,
Dressed like a pirate, he's quite the scare!
With a laugh, he declares a treasure quest,
But all that's buried is a big, fat jest.

They share the tales of the day gone by,
With hiccuped laughter and friendly sighs.
In the grove where silliness thrives,
Nature smiles as joy arrives.

Chronicles of the Grove

Once upon a time, in a leafy nook,
A bear read fortunes from an old book.
The mice all giggled, rolled on the floor,
When predicted tales caused quite a roar.

A turtle slow danced to a funky beat,
His moves were odd, but oh so sweet.
The armadillos joined with a spin,
Creating chaos as they laughed in chagrin.

The wise old owl, with spectacles on,
Told jokes so corny; he was never done.
The trees shook gently as they did sway,
In sync with the laughter, come what may.

At twilight's call, they shared their dreams,
Of marshmallow castles and gummy bear teams.
A final giggle, a sleepy goodbye,
Under twinkling stars, the night sighed.

Journey Through Leafy Labyrinths

In the maze of leaves, where shadows play,
A squirrel lost his way, oh what a day!
He asked a snail with a shell so bright,
Who chuckled softly, 'Just take a right!'

The hedgehogs rolled in a dizzy race,
Spinning in circles, what a silly chase!
With every tumble, giggles erupted,
As the path ahead constantly disrupted.

A parrot swooped down, squawking facts,
While the beetles debated the best snacks.
'An acorn here!' one beetle did cheer,
And off they went with a bumbling gear.

As stars peeked in with a twinkling wink,
The critters laughed, shared tales over drink.
Through leafy pathways, laughter expanded,
In this wild journey, all were happy, enchanted.

Secrets of the Silver Bark

Once trees told tales, with roots in the ground,
Squirrels held meetings; oh, what a sound!
Whispers of acorns and giggles so bright,
Mischief abounding from morn until night.

They plotted of pranks, of nutty delight,
Who'd steal the last snack? Oh, what a sight!
With branches a-swaying, they hatched wild plans,
Daring each other, these curious clans.

Sunlight would dance, as laughter would ring,
Banana peels slipped, oh, what joy they'd bring!
The wise old owl chuckled, a waggle of wings,
For secrets of mischief are what nature sings.

As twilight arrived, in shadows they'd roam,
Playing leapfrog with bushes—never a home!
Each night they'd gather, 'neath crescent moon mark,
Sharing the laughter beneath silver bark.

Underneath the Tranquil Canopy

Beneath leafy curtains, the critters would hide,
An otter named Ollie, with a smile so wide,
Declared it a day for a slip-and-slide show,
Down the slick mossy hill, they'd all go!

A raccoon named Ruby brought snacks for the crew,
With marshmallows flying and feathers, too.
All the birds fluttered, laughing in air,
As the scuffle ensued, with giggles to spare.

A turtle named Tom, in a hurry for fun,
Tripped over branches, saying, "I won!"
Laughter erupted; they rolled 'neath the leaves,
Knotted and tangled like yarn from the sleeves.

At dusk they'd all settle and share midnight tales,
Of frogs caught a-singing in muddy old trails.
With snickers and whispers in every last nook,
Underneath the canopy, they'd share their own book.

Enchanted Routes of Foliage

In the paths 'neath the ferns, a riddle took flight,
A chameleon named Charlie misjudged day and night.
He'd blend in with leaves, confused as could be,
Everywhere searching, but he couldn't see!

A hedgehog named Heidi rolled by with a grin,
"What's lost in the forest can never be seen!"
They giggled together, tangled in their quest,
An adventure in finding was surely the best.

As twigs snapped like crackers beneath tiny feet,
They ventured through mazes, perplexed but upbeat.
A rabbit named Benny made maps with old cheese,
Forgetting the route? Oh, what a tease!

With laughter as spice, they'd wander and chase,
Making each moment a curious race.
In enchanted routes, they stumbled and tripped,
But every good tussle just added to the script.

Echoes of the Emerald Forest

In the heart of the woods, where the echoes would play,
A frog named Freddy jumped high every day.
He'd croak out a tune that was catchy and loud,
Inviting all creatures to gather around.

The beavers brought drums made of wood and some pine,
They danced in a circle, their rhythm divine.
With flashes of tails and a splash of delight,
The forest became a grand stage for the night.

A skunk named Sally brought berries for snacks,
While squirrels would twirl with fancy young acts.
Together they painted the night with fresh cheer,
In echoes of laughter, they danced without fear.

As dawn's early light snuck through branches above,
They basked in the warmth of the memories of love.
In emerald hues, under skies painted blue,
The echoes of friendship made dreams come true.

The Spirit of the Spruce

In the forest where shadows play,
The Spruce cracks jokes, come what may.
With branches that wiggle and sway,
It whispers secrets, brightening the day.

A squirrel roasts nuts near its base,
Sharing laughs in the open space.
The Spruce tells tales of acorn race,
While pine cones dance in comical grace.

Even the roots chuckle and twine,
In this woodland where goofballs align.
Tree trunks hug with a twist so fine,
Laughs echo, a chorus divine.

So when you roam the wild and free,
Don't forget, it's all meant to be.
Join the Spruce, have a chuckle, you'll see,
Nature's humor is the key to glee!

Shielded by the Crowns

Beneath the boughs where birds sing loud,
A jester hat blades through a tree crowd.
Chirping squirrels pull stunts, so proud,
While crowns of leaves form a leafy shroud.

The branches stretch for a sky-high catch,
An acorn drops, causing quite a scratch.
The bark laughs hard, starts to dispatch,
A ruckus in rhythm, nature's own match.

A beetle in boots twirls with flair,
Mixing up dances with zest in the air.
Underneath giggles, they swish without care,
Chasing the breezes, the laughter they share.

Lost in the giggles, our hearts taking flight,
Beneath those crowns, everything feels right.
So come join the frenzy, from morn to night,
In a kingdom of chuckles and pure delight!

A Dance with the Dappled Green

A rabbit twirls on a leafy stage,
With daisies applauding, setting the gauge.
The dappled light is all the rage,
Come twist and twirl, break free from the cage.

Grass blades giggle, in sync they sway,
While frogs in tuxedos sing, "Hooray!"
Each step is a riddle, come what may,
In dappled green, they play the day away.

The squirrels juggle nuts, quite the show,
As butterflies flutter, with flair they glow.
The forest floor's a grand maestro,
Unleashing laughter, just like a pro.

And when twilight beckons with a soft hum,
The stars shimmy along, join the fun.
Dappled green dances, and even the drum,
Embabulate joy – they'll never succumb!

Of Rooted Dreams

In the soft soil where dreams take flight,
The roots murmur tales throughout the night.
Little plants giggle, in pure delight,
As worms hum tunes, bringing magic in sight.

With dew drops glistening like jolly beads,
The flowers bop as the night proceeds.
Each story woven, like woven reeds,
In the realm of roots, fun never concedes.

Amidst laughter, the night owl sprawls,
Winking at shadows that twirl and call.
Full of wisdom, it plucks the thralls,
To spin silly yarns, enthralling us all.

So lay on the grass, let your dreams roam free,
In rooted dreams, explore joy's decree.
From the soil to the stars, a wild jubilee,
Magic and laughter, life's sweet melody!

In the Realm of Rustling Leaves

In the realm where leaves do dance,
Squirrels plot a nutty prance.
With acorns flying through the air,
Watch that tree—it's a wild affair!

Raccoons wearing tiny hats,
Scheme in shadows, oh, what chitchats!
With lumberjack dreams in their eyes,
They'll build a fort where laughter flies.

A hedgehog slides down a muddy hill,
Belly flops give all a thrill.
The birds cheer on with a merry tune,
As frogs croak in the afternoon.

At sunset's blush, the fun won't stop,
They have a disco on the top!
With twinkling lights strung from trees,
They dance all night, carried by the breeze.

Treading Lightly Through Nature's Labyrinth

In nature's maze, we tread so light,
Dodging birds in playful flight.
The foxes giggle, tails in a swirl,
As butterflies dance, in a whirl!

An owl with glasses reads the rules,
While raccoons gather like clever fools.
One holds a map drawn in crayon,
And asks, 'Which way do we spawn?'

Through bushes thick and muddy trails,
A toad hops by, spinning tales.
A punch line here, a ribbit there,
Laughter echoes through the air.

By the river, they paddle their feet,
Dancing to the frogs' steady beat.
With nature's giggles in full swing,
They make the woods a joyous spring!

Fables from the Forest Floor

On the forest floor, tales spin and twirl,
Where mushrooms giggle and leaves unfurl.
The ants tell secrets of treasure they seek,
While crickets hold concerts twice a week!

A hedgehog's dance was quite absurd,
With twirls and spins, it's quite the word!
The rabbits cheer with snickers and squeals,
Admiring the charm of those spiky heels!

Mice in coats discuss etiquette fine,
While bumblebees buzz, "Oh, what a line!"
The breeze just chuckles, no need to rush,
In this fable-filled, whimsical hush.

As twilight draws close, a lullaby sings,
Amongst the whispers of the forest kings.
With frolicsome hearts and mischief galore,
The fables of nature forever roar!

Adventures in the Twisted Grove

In the twisted grove where shadows play,
A snail named Gary leads the way.
He boasts of speed, yet last I checked,
He stopped for lunch—oh, what the heck!

A twisty path of bumps and bends,
Where giraffe and penguin are unlikely friends.
With giggles loud and mischief planned,
They search for ice cream in this wild land!

A parrot squawks, "Adventure awaits!"
While a bunny negotiates with plates.
They argue over where the fun may hide,
With laughter spilling far and wide.

As twilight falls, fireflies glow,
The grove comes alive in a friendly show.
With stories shared and memories made,
In this wonderland, joy won't fade!

The Serpent's Path

In the bushes, a slithery fella,
Told a joke to a wise old cella.
It wiggled with glee,
And danced with a tree,
As the toads clapped like they were at Coachella.

A lizard bust out with a quirky twist,
Said, "I've got moves that you can't resist!"
They all took a chance,
In a scaled-up dance,
While birds dropped their snacks in a mist.

With each turn, the laughter grew loud,
Even the snake was starting to crowd.
They twirled and they spun,
'Til the day was all done,
Then slinked home to boast to the crowd.

So remember this tale, oh reader dear,
Of the serpents who danced without fear.
For the woods were alive,
With joy they had thrived,
And they left weeping willows with cheer.

Stillness in the Thicket

In the thicket, where stillness meets fun,
Lived a critter who thought he could run.
He tripped on a shoelace,
Made a tumble in place,
And laughed 'til he cried in the sun.

A squirrel with nuts thought it a grand show,
Joined the party, said, "Hey, watch me go!"
He spun in a circle,
Then slipped with a twirl,
Turned his stash into quite the grand throw!

A rabbit hopped in, with daring flair,
Said, "I can kick high, if you don't mind to stare!"
But he leaped with a yelp,
And forgot how to help,
Landed right in the fox's lair!

The thicket echoed with chirps and with laughs,
Those funny little woods held great gaffes.
A dance so absurd,
Not one creature stirred,
They rolled in the grass, no time for the halves.

Legends of the Leafy Realm

In a realm of green leaves, tales spun round,
Where acorns were kings and wisdom was found.
A beetle with glitter,
Grew tired of litter,
Said, "I'd rather be jiving than bound!"

He rallied the ants, who formed a parade,
With branches for trumpets and roots that they played.
They danced on a hill,
With nary a thrill,
While the lazy old snails just swayed.

A gossiping crow perched close on a limb,
Cawed stories of heroes and whimsy, not grim.
But then he went low,
And let out a crow,
The way he tripped over—oh, what a dim!

So remember the legends of laughter and joy,
Of beetles and ants, each girl and each boy.
For in leafy halls,
Where each creature sprawls,
They found that the fun was their greatest decoy.

Fever of the Fungi

In the woods where the mushrooms sprout high,
Lived a thumping old toad with a gleamy eye.
He twirled with great glee,
Said, "Join in with me!"
And the fungi began jumping like they'd fly!

A ladybug laughed, with spots shining bright,
She joined in, her rhythm a silly delight.
With a hop and a skip,
And a very big flip,
They took the whole forest to new heights!

The ground shook with laughter, the trees swayed with cheer,
As the mushrooms all hummed a tune loud and clear.
The snails moved in packs,
In their own funky tracks,
While the fireflies buzzed in a circle so near.

So next time you find a wild pop-up shroom,
Just remember the party that lit up the gloom.
With a giggle and hop,
And a non-stop bop,
You too can join in and dispel all the doom.

Upon the Canopy's Edge

Up high where squirrels play,
A bird drops snacks all day.
I try to catch them mid-flight,
But end up in quite a sight.

Mice scamper in tiny shoes,
Stealing crumbs, it's such bad news.
I'd chase them with a laugh so loud,
But trip and fall, oh, I'm so proud!

Branches wave like arms in cheer,
While rabbits hop without a fear.
I join their dance, oh what a show,
But faceplant softly, much to my woe.

As sunlight streams through leafy hues,
I lose my way, oh what a cruise!
Adventure calls, I take a dive,
Into the bushes—oops! I'm alive!

Tales Woven in Woodland Whispers

There's gossip in the prickly bramble,
Of fairies that trip and sometimes gamble.
With acorn hats, oh what a sight,
They laugh at me, oh, what a fright!

A deer with specs reads from a book,
Saying, 'Can you please not step on the nook?'
I promise him it's truly my goal,
To read with him, just can't find the scroll.

Beneath a mushroom, a picnic's spread,
With ants as waiters, they don't tread.
I ask for cheese, they look confused,
They bring me crumbs, how dare they refuse!

In whispers, trees share secrets anew,
Of a raccoon's hat or the owl's view.
Each laughter echoes through the night,
As stars wink down, all feelings are bright!

Heartbeats in the Hallowed Grove

In the grove where shadows play,
A fox is dancing in a fray.
With twirls and spins, he shows his flair,
But trips on roots, oh dear—beware!

The owls hoot in silly tones,
While crickets chirp in mellow drones.
A moonlit party, full of glee,
Yet I step right on a bumblebee!

Branches hang low, tickle my nose,
I sneeze like thunder, oh how it goes!
The crowd of critters leaps in fear,
A tickled tree falls, what a leer!

In this grove, we laugh and play,
As raccoons juggle under a bouquet.
It's harmony in foolish acts,
With woodland friends, no need for pacts!

Navigating Nature's Hidden Corridors

I wander down winding paths of green,
Where mossy carpets softly glean.
With every twist and turn, I shout,
But watch my step—I stubbed my clout!

A hedgehog grins, with spiky hair,
As I blindly crash into his lair.
He laughs and rolls, then darts away,
Leaving me in fits of dismay!

In the thicket, thorns make their play,
I dance and prance, but can't delay.
The bushes whisper, "This way's best!"
I follow, yet end up in a nest!

Through corridors of leaves I run,
Chasing shadows, oh what fun!
With laughter echoing in the breeze,
Nature's puzzles put me at ease!

Flight of the Squirrel

A squirrel took off, what a sight,
Leaping from branches, oh what a flight!
With acorns in tow, he danced in the air,
Chasing his shadow like he didn't care.

He twirled with a twist, almost a show,
Flipping through leaves, a furry tornado,
He landed on one, right by my shoe,
Squinting his eyes like he knew what to do.

Then off he raced, a blur in the green,
With a tail like a flag, his victory seen,
But tripped on a root, oh what a plight,
Falling in style, oh what a delight!

He shook off the dust with a grand, silly flair,
No harm in his tumble, he just had to share,
Up the tree he went, so wild and free,
"Catch me if you can!" was his only decree.

Colors of the Seasonal Shift

Leaves turned to gold, then crimson they gleam,
Dancing on branches like a fevered dream,
A pumpkin, a squash, all jumbled and bright,
Nature's own palette, a riotous sight.

Squirrels are stirring, with nuts they conspire,
Hoarding their treasures, their little quagmire,
Jumping and scurrying, all through the day,
Planning their feasts in a nutty ballet.

Oh, how they chatter in fall's crisp embrace,
Rivalry blooms in this colorful race,
Falling from trees, they embrace the surprise,
As winds lift the leaves, they flutter and fly.

And when winter strikes, oh the chaos will brew,
With snowflakes a-flutter, their antics anew,
In coats of bright laughter, they'll romp and they'll play,
These jesters of autumn, come what may!

Ribbons of Light

Sunbeams spilling down like ribbons of gold,
Through branches they weave, a story untold,
Critters chuckling beneath leafy glee,
What mischief awaits in this shimmering spree?

The shadows do tango, a light-hearted dance,
Dappled and freckled, they spin and they prance,
A squirrel twirls 'round like a seasoned old pro,
Till he trips on a twig, what a comical show!

Butterflies flutter with giggles and flares,
Tickling the flowers as if they were pears,
Jumping from blooms in delightful delight,
Painting the woods in a festival bright.

So what's the lesson in this waltz of the sun?
Life's just better when you're having some fun,
Join in the frolic, let your heart take flight,
In the dance of the forest, all is just right.

The Forest's Breath

In the hush of the morn, the forest awakes,
With whispers of laughter, and high-flying pranks,
A raccoon in pajamas, stretching with yawns,
Slippers of moss on his little, big paws.

Tweetles and chirps, oh what a grand choir,
The woodpecker's tap, like a beat on a wire,
While beavers get busy, with sticks on parade,
Building their dams with such crafty charade.

The breeze brings a chuckle, it swirls and it sways,
Tickling the giants with playful delays,
A fox flips a leaf with a pounce and a grin,
As mischief abounds in this numerical din.

So dwell in the woods, let your heart find its glee,
In the laughs and the dances, wild and carefree,
For every small creature knows just how to please,
In the forest, dear friend, there's joy like the breeze.

Tales of the Treetops

In the high branches, we swing and sway,
Giggling as squirrels throw acorns our way.
A parrot squawks jokes, quite absurd,
We laugh 'til we tumble, not a bit disturbed.

A raccoon joins in with a dance so grand,
Wobbling on branches, it's all quite unplanned.
We cheer him on, though he stumbles a bit,
It's a wild party, every critter unfit.

The wind tells stories, they twist and they twine,
Of tree-top mishaps, and cookies divine.
We feast on strange fruits, with giggles abound,
As the pranks of the forest spin round and round.

Under the moonlight, we play hide and seek,
From owls who hoot and the tiny mouse squeak.
In the treetops so high, we've found quite a crew,
Adventure awaits, and we've plenty to do!

Lullabies of the Leafy Canopy

Sleepy squirrels snuggle in leafy embrace,
While bouncy frogs leap in a rhythm and race.
A sloth sings softly, with a drawl so slow,
His lullabies drift through the breezy flow.

The moon laughs brightly, catching fireflies' lights,
As chipmunks tell tales of their wild, wacky nights.
Caught in the branches, a mischief of bees,
Bumble just to bother, with giggles and wheezes.

A wise old owl hoots a tune so absurd,
Whiskers twitching, it's both silly and blurred.
We sway to his song, in a blanket of stars,
Dreams of wild antics and comical sparrs.

With branches like pillows, we secretly scheme,
To wake woodland creatures, to join in our dream.
In the leafy canopy, laughter rings clear,
As the forest becomes our playground, my dear!

In Search of the Elusive Glade

We march through the forest, a crew on a quest,
Seeking a glade where the sun shines the best.
A bear offers snacks and a fox leads the way,
Who knew that adventures could start with a play?

Then over the hill, a strange rustle, we hear,
It's a turtle, who's lost, in a whirl of good cheer.
"Join us," we shout, as he takes off his hat,
He spins in a circle, how silly is that?

Through tickling tall grass, we giggle and run,
A hedgehog spins tales of the best kind of fun.
"More berries!" we call, as they tumble around,
Magic moments and laughter are easily found.

At last, we discover the glade of our dreams,
Waving to bumblebees and shining moonbeams.
With a daisy crown, we declare it our place,
In the heart of the forest, we've found our grace!

Adventures Between the Twigs

Our adventures begin with a twig as our guide,
It wiggles and wiggles while we laugh in pride.
A lizard popped up, offering us bets,
Who could leap further? Oh, what fun it begets!

We twist and we turn, like a dance in the air,
While ants march proudly without a single care.
They wave tiny flags, directing their crew,
As we cheer them on, with a giggle or two.

Then comes a rabbit, with tales oh so tall,
A chase with a hare? Come one, come all!
With hops and with skips, we dash through the green,
To discover the wonders yet to be seen.

As dusk softly whispers, our games start to slow,
With twigs as our treasure, we bask in the glow.
In this fine forest, with friends all around,
The best of adventures is where joy is found!

Voices in the Twilight

In the dusk, the whispers blend,
Squirrels gossip, my ears they send.
With tiny pies and nuts in sight,
They argue over who baked right.

A raccoon dances, thinks he's suave,
While fireflies buzz, a starlit rave.
Nature's party, no invitation,
But everyone joins the celebration!

An owl hoots, with wisdom he brags,
While frogs croak out their karaoke jags.
Beetles break out in a rhythmic spin,
While the hedgehogs roll, they can't help but grin.

And as moonlight pulls the curtain tight,
All creatures share their silly plight.
In the twilight, laughter ignites,
A symphony of comical delights.

Solitude in the Thicket

Amid tall grass, I sit and sigh,
A lizard leaps, don't know why.
In solitude, I ponder deep,
A tumbleweed comes, trying to creep.

A butterfly flutters, takes a break,
Announcing itself, a fluttering quake.
It flops and flutters with such flair,
While I'm stuck in this chair, with a stare.

A mouse scurries past with cheese in tow,
He twitches like a star in a show.
I wave hello, he squeaks back loud,
While ants form lines, so very proud.

Then branches crack, and what a sight!
A hedgehog rolls, oh, what a fright!
Together we laugh—my woodland crew,
In solitude, I found a zoo.

Enchantment of the Woods

In the woods, where shadows play,
A squirrel shouts, "Hey, it's my day!"
He spins in circles, chases his tail,
While a chipmunk tells a tall tale.

The leaves do chuckle, rustle like mad,
While a porcupine looks half sad.
"Ouch! Those thorns!" they yell in glee,
As my shoe laces tangle, oh dear me!

A dancing brook sings, 'Skip on a stone!'
While frogs leap high, claiming each throne.
Magic swirls in this forest dance,
With critters, I twirl—I've found my chance!

And when twilight drapes its silky veil,
Fireflies blink, a shimmering trail.
With all the giggles and joy they impart,
This enchanted wood steals every heart.

Lost Among Rain-Drenched Roots

With puddles splashing, I leap and bound,
Muddied feet—oh look, a mound!
A worm peeks out, he tries to hide,
As raindrops laugh, 'Come take a ride!'

A slippy slope, I take my chance,
While frogs do jig in a rainy dance.
"Hey, you!" I shout, "This isn't fair!"
They croak back, "Join the slippery affair!"

I trip on roots, go crashing down,
And land in mud, the squishiest town.
A hedgehog chuckles, "Is this your fate?"
As I squirm in joy, don't hesitate.

But in the chaos, laughter roars,
Nature's antics open its doors.
And in the rain, I find delight,
Lost in laughter, my spirit takes flight.

Wandering with the Wild

On a quest with a squirrel named Lou,
We chased after a duck in a shoe.
He quacked and he flapped, it was quite the sight,
As we stumbled and tumbled till the dark night.

A raccoon joined, wearing a hat,
He tried to juggle, but fell on his mat.
We laughed 'til we cried, what a silly show,
Underneath the trees where the wild things grow.

The owl hooted, 'What a goofy train!'
As we danced in circles, forgetting the rain.
With twirls and flops, we made quite a scene,
In the woods where adventure reigns supreme.

Finally collapsed, in a heap, we lay,
With dreams of tomorrow's wacky play.
For in the wild, each day is a gift,
With friends like these, our spirits will lift.

Tales from the Timberline

A pinecone fell and knocked me down,
"What a way to greet the town!"
With giggles echoing through the trees,
I brushed off dirt and yelled, "More, please!"

A chipmunk danced in tap shoes bright,
While a moose played trumpet, what a delight!
The crowd of critters all clapped their paws,
For this woodland band played without flaws.

They served up snacks from an acorn dish,
"Just one more bite," said the greedy fish.
We feasted 'til dusk on berries and stew,
"What a feast in the forest!" we all cheered, "Woo-hoo!"

As stars twinkled in the darkened sky,
We told tall tales, letting laughter fly.
In the timberline, adventure is grand,
With a band of friends, it's perfectly planned.

Moonlight Among the Branches

Under the moon with a glow so bright,
A band of raccoons took to flight.
They zipped and they zed in the pale moonlight,
Trying to catch fireflies, quite the sight!

A rabbit hopped in, asking for tips,
"Can you teach me to dance without any flips?"
The raccoons laughed as they spun in the air,
While the rabbit just tumbled without a care.

Meanwhile, an owl gave his wise old glare,
"Keep it down, folks, we must beware!"
But with a wink, he joined in the fun,
Hooping and hollering, one by one.

As dawn neared, their antics slowed,
With sleepy smiles, they shared the load.
For under the moon, laughter ran free,
Just a night in the woods, as fun as can be.

Nature's Clockwork Symphony

Tick-tock said the squirrel, munching on a nut,
As a badger joined with a honking strut.
A clockwork world where all things play,
In rhythms and beats that brightens the day.

The leaves rustled, keeping time,
While frogs croaked in perfect rhyme.
Even the breeze hummed a happy tune,
As flowers danced, swaying under the moon.

A butterfly added a fluttering beat,
While a hedgehog tapped, oh so neat.
The forest rang with a fanciful cheer,
As critters joined in, bringing joy near.

When sunset came, they took a bow,
With yawns and grins, "Oh my, what a show!"
In nature's symphony, laughter is bright,
In a world of fun, where all feels just right.

A Path Less Traveled

Two squirrels plotted under the tree,
Carting acorns, laughing with glee.
One slipped and fell, mud flew in the sky,
They both burst out laughing, oh my, oh my!

They found a path, so narrow and wild,
With twists and turns, like a playful child.
A frog jumped out, startled and keen,
"Why are you here? This is my green!"

A rabbit joined in, with a twitching nose,
"Join our race, and heaven knows!"
They ran and tumbled, in a carefree spree,
Until they crashed right into a bee!

The bee buzzed loud, "What's all the fuss?"
In the chaos, they formed a bus.
With acorns as seats, they sailed through the air,
On a path less traveled, without a care!

Mysteries of the Mossy Knoll

At the mossy knoll where shadows dance,
A gnome led a parade, not a chance!
With mismatched socks and a lopsided hat,
They marched on forward, looking a spat!

A toad had a baton, green and slimy,
Conducting a band that played so primy.
The trees swayed along in rhythmic delight,
While the bugs held a concert deep in the night.

An owl hooted loud, "What's the ruckus here?"
The gnome just winked, "Bring us your cheer!"
The owl rolled its eyes, but joined the show,
As the moonlight twinkled with a soft, golden glow.

From under the ferns, a raccoon peered,
"Can I join in?" It slyly sneered.
With laughter and music, the knoll was alive,
Where mysteries lurked, and joy would thrive!

The Surreal Soundscape

In a world where the flowers could talk,
And every leaf held a secret walk,
A snail played the flute with a kind of grace,
While the sunbeams danced round in jubilant race.

A caterpillar crooned a wobbly tune,
As clouds drifted by, shaped like a spoon.
Amidst the giggles of whispers so light,
The trees swayed and shouted, "What a delight!"

A fish in the sky wore a bright yellow hat,
"Tell me, dear friends, what's the matter with that?"
It flopped in the air, making quite the splash,
While crickets provided a giddy, quick crash.

With rainbows of sound, they painted the day,
In a surreal landscape, where giggles would stay.
And if you listen close, you might hear the song,
Of a world full of laughter, where all can belong!

Beneath the Wavering Limbs

Beneath the branches that danced in the breeze,
A family of ants held a feast with great ease.
They served tiny crumbs and spilled some sweet jam,
While debating the best way to ready a plan!

A grasshopper jumped in with a joke so tight,
"Why did the leaf refuse to take flight?"
The ants all chuckled with cheeks full of treats,
"Because it wasn't ready to hit the cool streets!"

A caterpillar waved, spinning tales of his past,
Of the time he got lost, but found home at last.
With each little story, they giggled and sighed,
In their lively realm, where no one has cried.

So under those limbs, they sang through the night,
With laughter and joy, everything felt right.
A place where the silly could happily roam,
Beneath the waving limbs, they all felt at home!

Life's Tapestry in Green

In the forest where squirrels plot,
A rabbit forgot what it ought.
He hopped over logs, oh what a sight,
Chased by a snail, moving with might.

Vines tangled up with giggles and glee,
A raccoon discovered my lost shoe, you see!
With hats made of leaves, they danced on the breeze,
While bees played the drums, swaying with ease.

The trees whispered secrets, oh what a fuss,
Telling tales of a skunk who rode on a bus.
With acorns as tickets, he traveled afar,
Singing loud tunes under the evening star.

So here in the green, the world feels alive,
Where laughter and nature together thrive.
Join in the fun, no need for a plan,
For every day's a new sketch from the clan.

Guardian of the Glades

A lizard in armor holds court on a log,
In charge of the critters, the hen and the frog.
He shouts, "Spread the word, a feast is in sight!"
With berries and crumbs for a sweet, silly night.

The hedgehog, the bard, recites a fine tale,
Of a snail who dreamed of sailing a sail.
With cardboard and twine, he built quite a ship,
Yet forgot to tie down, and took a strange trip.

The owls hoot in chorus, "What's that in the sky?"
A wayward raccoon with a pie, oh my!
The guardian sighs as he rolls his sharp eyes,
But laughter erupts under moonlit skies.

In this whimsical world, even shadows can play,
Where nonsense reigns, come join in the fray.
Let giggles ignite 'neath a marvelous moon,
For mischief and laughter forever in tune.

Ephemeral Hazards

Watch out for the puddles, they jump with delight,
As frogs leap for joy in a splashing big fight.
A squirrel slips by on a skateboard so slick,
And crashes into flowers, it's a humorous trick.

Grasshoppers challenge on hops and on jumps,
As bugs cheer and gather in huddled-up clumps.
A tumbleweed rolls, all tumbleweed great,
Spinning round, causing a jitterbug fate.

The wisest of turtles winks at the scene,
While butterflies laugh, gleaming bright and serene.
"Adventure awaits! Keep your wits about!"
But the raccoon just snickered, rolling about.

With each little blunder, we learn how to steer,
Through breezy mishaps, let out a cheer.
For here in this moment, we dance and we sway,
In a world full of giggles, come join the ballet!

Home Among the Blossoms

In a garden where daisies peek out from the earth,
A bumblebee grumbles, "What's all this worth?"
He's stuck in a flower, too big for his frame,
And all of us chuckle, we're not one to blame.

The daisies nod gently, spreading bright cheer,
As a butterfly flutters, drawing near.
"Oh, what a place for a tea party spree!"
With crumbs from the hedges, we gather with glee.

A gopher in shades hands out tiny drinks,
While ants on a mission work faster than kinks.
"Do bring more snacks!" he pleas, quite out of breath,
A feast for our crew, not even a bone left.

So here in this bloom, where laughter prevails,
With giggles and snacks, and some funny tales.
In the heart of the blossoms, we call it our home,
In gardens of joy, together we roam.

Beneath the Embrace of Twisted Roots

Beneath the ground where whispers hide,
A raccoon wears a hat, looking dignified.
He tips it low, in a comical stance,
While squirrels gather, planning their dance.

Mushrooms giggle as they grow in clusters,
Chasing each other like little jesters.
They tickle the toes of a pine so stout,
Who simply grumbles, shedding his route.

A rabbit hops in, holding a cup,
Sipping moonlight—says he's all up!
The roots are tangled, laughter ensues,
While owls play poker, they can't lose!

With every twist, a joyfully muddled sight,
The forest breathes with humorous delight.
In this lively realm of playful cheers,
Even the shadows break into jeers.

The Call of the Forest Spirits

In the heart of the woods, a scarecrow sings,
Joking with fireflies, sharing their wings.
A ghostly tree with a toothy grin,
Challenging critters to spin and spin.

Fairies argue over who makes the best brew,
While a badger declares he's winning too.
Sparks fly as laughter echoes around,
In this wild place where giggles abound.

A bear juggles honey, gets sticky and stuck,
As raccoons declare, 'It's a funny old luck!'
With spirits of nature, all joys collide,
As trees come alive, full of mischief and pride.

So heed the call of the playful throng,
Join in the fun, you can't go wrong!
In the dance of the leaves and stars that ignite,
Every moment's a jest—oh what a sight!

Lost in the Lush Wilderness

Wandering deep in the thickest brush,
Stumbled upon a silly rush.
A turtle plays tag with a leaping hare,
While vibrant blooms gossip without a care.

Frogs wear crowns, commencing a show,
With choreography no one should know.
They leap and croak, each step a delight,
While crickets orchestrate a symphony bright.

A family of deer prances, a graceful parade,
As a fox sneezes, and chaos invades.
With foliage twisting, laughter won't cease,
In this kingdom of whimsy, all feelings increase.

So when you're lost, you may just find,
The funniest friends by being unlined.
In the lush wilderness, oh what a cheer,
Embrace the comical, allow them near!

The Hidden Glades of Reverie

In a glade where shadows break into song,
The bushes debate who's right and wrong.
A porcupine rants in a witty display,
While bees buzz around in a humorous fray.

Hidden treasures of laughter abound,
As raccoons drum on the soft ground.
They chuckle and tumble, in fits of delight,
Making mischief till the fall of night.

A hedgehog mistaken for a rolling ball,
Crashes the party, but stands oh so tall.
With pinecones wearing hats, spinning around,
Every step taken leads to tales profound.

So if you wish to roam the green sea,
Remember the jesters waiting for thee.
In hidden glades where laughter creates,
The mirth of the woods simply radiates!

www.ingramcontent.com/pod-product-compliance
Lightning Source LLC
Chambersburg PA
CBHW072137200426
43209CB00050B/68